J'AIME MA .BLEUETTE.

THE DOLLS AND COSTUMES OF BLEUETTE AND FRIENDS

BY FLORENCE THERIAULT

& NELLY FARGE-THERIAULT

To order additional copies contact:
Dollmasters
PO Box 2319
Annapolis, MD 21404
Tel. 800-966-3655, Fax 410-571-9605
www.dollmasters.com

This book is based upon the Private Collection of Madame X of Paris, France auctioned by Theriault's of Annapolis, Maryland.

Design by Travis Hammond
Photography by Gerald Nelson

$39
ISBN: 1-931503-30-3
Printed in Hong Kong

FOREWORD

Although Paris-born Bleuette has been around for 100 years (1905-2005), she remained mostly apart from American shores until the late years of the 20 th century. All that has changed. Bleuette is now the hot new kid on the American block, and even as growing bands of collectors surge to befriend Bleuette, there are others wondering what the hullabaloo is all about.

Bleuette was born as a publicity offer. Take a subscription to the new French children's journal *La Semaine de Suzette* and earn a doll. The doll offered during its initial year, 1905, was a classic Jumeau model that was being made at this time by SFBJ, but so successful was the promotion that 20,000 dolls were sold out – presto! By 1917, Bleuette had become so successful that the owners, Gautier and Languereau, began to create actual costumes for the dolls, rather than simply offer patterns. These costumes were presented for sale in *La Semaine de Suzette*, and in a semi-annual costume catalog that they published for the next 40 years. From that time forward the dolls and costumes could be at the Gautier-Languereau offices in Paris, or could be mail-ordered throughout French, its colonies, and "pays etrangers". These "pays etrangers" apparently included America although there is no historical indication that the dolls were ever played with by American children during this time. The market for French dolls was largely finished in America after the early 1920's and American children had turned to their own popular culture dress-up dolls ranging from Patsy to Ginny.

A study of the Bleuette catalogs is a most useful primer on changing 20th century fashions. Because the catalogs were illustrated by well-known French artists, many of whom were famous for their drawings in the Etrennes catalogs of the Paris department stores of that time, it is possible to see the costumes as the designers imaged them – the hat perched just so on the head, the proper shoes to wear with each dress, the way the dress should drape. That the costumes never did exactly fit the dolls as the illustrators drew them did nothing to discourage the young dreamers who played with them. The catalogs, when found today, provide an incredible store of knowledge, naming the colors and fabric designs of each costume, and the fabric type, and the social occasion where the costume would be appropriately worn. And because, generally speaking, the costumes appeared for one season only, they present a highly specific passing scene of fashion.

The catalogs are also useful in judging the rarity of a costume. It is reasonable to assume that the earliest documented costumes are the rarest. It is reasonable to assume that more expensive costumes are more rare than budget dresses. It is reasonable to assume that certain fragile fabrics stood up poorly and thus are rare.

The catalogs do provide another tantalizing piece of information. At the time when young girls could own either the doll or costume or both, what was most expensive? Yes, (with few exceptions) it was the costume. Bleuette, herself, was merely the lure. To Gautier-Languereau, the costumes were the feast. In view of that, it is surprising that today's collectors have focused so intently on minor nuances of the doll description, arguing for hours "is she or isn't she?" about each Bleuette model, rather than pursuing a thorough appreciation of the costumes.

Emulation is the sincerest form of flattery in all things, and so it is with dolls. The idea of a standard size doll with a vast choice of trousseau was neither novel nor uncommon. There was the classic 45 cm poupée "Lily" promoted by Madame Lavalle-Peronne and the ensuring offerings of costumes presented in her doll shop and in her journal, *La Poupée Modele*, designed to precisely fit that body. Lily was actually a standard generic poupée, and lovely as she was, her head could be one of several different models. It was her size and the style of her body that was key. The concept was a winner and other doll makers followed along. Soon there was a great array of standard 45 cm fashion dolls, and today's collector can only distinguish the "real" Lily by those few examples that have the original paper body label.

As for Bleuette, how does one distinguish the real thing from the type? Authorities dispute the credentials of the little dolls, but some facts are absolute. One absolute fact is the size. This size factor would have been important to Gautier-Languereau as it dictated the proportions of the costume, and, in fact, the number signed bodies are a good proof of that importance.

There is more dispute concerning the facial models and markings and what can be designated, without any question, as an all-original Bleuette. Certain models are accepted by all researchers. Other markings are considered to be Bleuette dolls by some collectors, but not by others Then there is the case of the Bleuette-sized SFBJ 251 character – is this from the Bleuette family or not? The argument is not likely to be settled soon. There are no Gautier-Languereau records located at this time that positively state what the markings on the head should be, another indication that the firm was more concerned with the size and style of the body than the model of the head.

What's a collector to do? Collectors, it seems, have made their own decision, collecting Bleuettes with unproven genealogy with the same zeal as they collect documented Bleuettes. Appeal, charm, and of course, the requisite size and standard body are of utmost importance. Knowledgeable collectors have begun to realize that it's all rather like Jumeau bébés: the early years are largely undocumented concerning markings on the head, the later years are well-documented and marked, and then there are all the mystery models, the yet-to-be-documented bébés that appeared throughout the firm's history.

So, why Bleuette in the American market? Certainly there is no nostalgia because Bleuette was not part of the American culture during her lifetime. Perhaps, as some say, she is just a fad. But there is another reason. The doll, who lived from 1905 until 1960, lived through two World Wars, the Roaring 20's, the Depression, the Occupation, and the 50's Rebirth. She lived through decades of fashionable change in the most fashion-conscious city in the world, and through decades of fabric change – from lace and silk to rayon to nylon. Her costumes and coiffes and accessories are all a reflection of these changing times, and aside from the pure fun of "playing with Bleuette" there is the concept of Bleuette as a vivid document of the social life of the Western world in the first half of the 20th century.

It's a curious side note that America's 20th century fashion doll, Barbie, came to life the very year before Bleuette ended. Put together, these two icon dolls and their fashion collections can provide for historians a century-long view of changing fashions and life styles. How fitting that America's Barbie is so very popular in France, and now, France's Bleuette has found a new home in America.

1. Bleuette, with bisque socket head, blue glass sleep eyes, mohair lashes, original Bleuette wig and pate, composition jointed body. The doll, 27 cm., is marked "Unis France 60 71 149 8/0" on the head, "2" on torso, and "1" on feet, and is wearing an original Bleuette costume from the 1950 era, similar to "Fleur des Champs" of the Summer 1955 catalog. The dress is of peach rayon printed with colorful field flowers and has an organdy collar, along with Bleuette straw bonnet, chemise, socks, and brown leather shoes marked "2". The doll is from the 1925 era. $1200/1700

2. "Premiere Valse", the two-piece ensemble appeared as #33 in the Spring/Summer 1957 catalog, comprising a raspberry-colored striped full-length cortege dress with flocked white dots, decorated with sienna velvet bow at the waist, with a matching cap having shirred edging. $300/400

3. "Mille Raies", the dress appeared as #5 in the Summer 1939 catalog, described as an "elegant little dress of crepe de chine", patterned with a rainbow of colors, with orange twill skirt border and waist sash. $300/400

4. Bleuette with trunk and trousseau. The doll has bisque socket head, blue glass sleep eyes, mohair lashes, mohair wig, pate, composition jointed body. The doll, 27 cm, is marked "Unis France 60 71 149 8/0" on the head, "2" on the torso, and "1" on the feet, and is presented in an original Bleuette trunk with a variety of original Gautier-Languereau costumes from the 1935-1950's era: muslin slip, socks and brown leather original shoes, "Premiere Valse" gown, "Uniforme" dress with belt and hat (no band), blue navy coat with two brass buttons, and cotton school dress. Bleuette is from the 1925 era. $2000/2500

5. Original Bleuette Catalog, Spring/Summer 1922. The eight page catalog lists and illustrates the new costumes of Bleuette offered by Gautier-Languereau for that season, and describes the two variations of Bleuette, "une jolie Poupée-Jumeau," that are available: with set eyes for 8.50 FF, or with sleep eyes for 10 FF. Wigs were available in three colors. $200/300

6. "Féerie", the dress appeared as #32 in the Winter 1958/1959 catalog and Summer 1959 catalog, made of pink organza with delicate white stripes, decorative band and bow on the full-length skirt. $300/400

7. "A L'Opéra", the dress appeared as #15 in the 1956/1957 catalog, made of turquoise blue soft velvet with self belt, white soutache trim on collar and cuffs. $200/300

8. "Contraste", the dress appeared in the Winter 1949/1950 catalog, made of linen-like pink cotton with blue skirt border and blue collar and belt. $200/250

9. "Sur Mon 31", the dress appeared as #5 in the Summer 1937 catalog, of pale blue/grey textured silk with self belt decorated with embroidery stitches. Small spot on skirt. $150/200

10. White sleeveless rayon dress with ribbed pattern and blue dots, trimmed with royal blue silk banding, with matching bolero jacket. Unidentified, circa 1920's. $100/150

11. "Sur Mon 31", from the Winter 1948/1949 catalog described as rose wool with tucks on the bodice, detachable belt with silver buckle, white organdy collar. Small hole in skirt. $300/400

12. "Cinq Heures", from the Winter 1954/1955 catalog, described as an elegant tasteful dress, of white wool patterned with red dots and red silk-like banding at the neckline, self sash. $200/300

13. White cotton dress with delicate pattern of abstract blue outlined flowers, V-shaped lace outline on bodice, double row of lace on skirt. Unidentified, circa 1930. $100/150

14. "Champs Elysées", from Winter 1953/1954 catalog, of blue rayon with white abstract pattern with blue button at front bodice. The dress was designed to be worn with coat, #218 in this book. $200/300

15. "Gala", the evening dress appeared as #19 in the Summer 1954 catalog, made of pale blue/grey faille decorated with silver metallic braid. $200/300

16. Original Bleuette catalog for Summer 1918, comprising four pages of costumes, Bleuette information and publicity. $200/300

17. "Stella", featured on the cover of the 1918 Gautier-Languereau catalog, the chic party dress of delicate patterned silk has a flapper style tunic blouse of blue crepe; the tunic and skirt are edged with tiny beads. Some frailty to left back panel of under-bodice. $900/1200

18. Peach rayon and tulle party dress with brocade rayon sleeveless bodice and three-tiered tulle ruffled skirt. The costume is unidentified but an identical model is shown in a group photograph of Bleuette dolls on exhibition in Hilliker's *Bleuette*, page 135. 1920's. $400/500

19. "Matinal", the ensemble appeared in the Spring/Summer 1924 catalog, comprising a skirt with attached cotton bodice and jacket of blue duvetine, with four decorative buttons. Along with blue straw toque decorated with "pompon fantaisie". $800/1000

20. "Frou-Frou", the bonnet first appeared in La Semaine de Suzette in 1915, and in the Winter 1916/1917 catalog, made of white cotton cutwork with stiffened lining for shape, tatting edge, aqua silk bows and trim, and white fabric flowers at each side. $300/400

21. "Nivose", the bonnet appeared as #101 in the Winter 1922 catalog, made of blue velvet with white plush border and trimmed with aqua and white cord. Overall dusty. $150/200

22. Blue Velour Bonnet, made of soft aqua blue velour with stitch-shaped body, turned back trim, blue silk ribbons, lining; unidentified. $150/200

23. Premiere Bleuette, with bisque socket head, brown glass inset eyes, painted lashes and brush-stroked brows, open mouth, four teeth, pierced ears, blonde mohair wig, cork pate, composition fully-jointed body. The 27 cm doll is marked "1" on the head, "2" on the back torso, and "1" on the feet, and owns an original chemise de nuit. Along with an antique handmade dress based upon "Robe de Casino" pattern in La Semaine de Suzette of 1905/1906, along with matching bonnet, socks and black leatherette shoes. Circa 1905. $4500/6500

26. "Allure", the dress appeared in the Winter 1954/1955 catalog, made of soft blue velvet with V-shaped bodice, frou-frou trim at neckline and sleeves, and detachable belt. Overall dustiness. $150/200

27. "Allure", identical to #26 except made of rich red velvet in vibrant color. $200/300

24. "Au Concert", the dress appeared as costume #1 in the Winter 1938/1939 catalog described as "robe blanche de soierie brochée", with red velvet sash and collar, and decorative buttons. $200/300

25. Chapeau with wide brim of intricately woven blue straw, very full cap of stiffened muslin with silk lining. Unidentified, from the 1920 era. $300/400

21. CANASTA

Robe très souple en foulard à petits trèfles sur fond jaune, bleu ou rouge .... **310** fr.

★

22. MONDANITÉS

BLEUETTE revient d'un mariage élégant dans sa longue robe d'organdi fileté ciel, rouge ou vert sur fond blanc. Capeline de même tissu. Les deux pièces pour .. **450** fr.

★

23. ALLURE

Modèle à succès cette robe de velours uni rouge ou roy, garnie d'un croquet blanc d'organdi ... **390** fr.

★

FARNIENTE

Un fauteuil transatlantique pliable.. **470** fr. Port et emballage en sus.......... **100** fr.

(voir ce modèle (page 15)

7

28. "Au Concert", the dress appeared as #11 in the Winter 1952/1953 catalog, made of rich red velvet garnished with "tuyauté de mousseline blanche". $200/300

29. "Au Concert", identical to #28, except of periwinkle blue velvet. $200/300

30. MONDANITES

Robe longue de cérémonie, en organdi fileté ciel, rouge ou vert sur fond blanc. Capeline de même tissu. Les deux pièces. **450** fr.

★

31. JEUNESSE

Toilette juvénile en toile soyeuse, fond blanc dessins roses ou rouges. Col-pèlerine bordé de croquet. **315** fr.

★

32. FLEUR DES CHAMPS

Cette robe de « MIGALINE » a toute la fraîcheur d'un bouquet champêtre. Jupe en corolle, légère collerette d'organdi plissé. **350**fr.

10

Opposite page: "Allure" shown in 1954 catalog of Gautier-Languereau.

Left: "Mondanites" shown in 1955 catalog of Gautier-Languereau.

30. "Mondanites", the costume appeared in the Summer, 1955 catalog, of pink nylon patterned with pink and white horizontal stripes, with four crystal-like plastic buttons, self belt, fitted cuffs, and lined collar. $200/300

31. Brown velvet sateen dress printed with small cream design, front pleat, bretelle sleevelets, white round collar. Although unidentified, the costume is certainly Gautier-Languereau of the 1930 era. $300/400

32. Original Bleuette catalog of Summer 1933, with cover illustration by artist Maggie Salcedo who designed many covers of French department store catalogs during the 1920's and 1930's, has twelve pages of costumes and scenes. $200/300

33. "Parisienne", the two-piece ensemble appeared as costume #1 in the Winter 1937/1938 catalog, comprising a green velvet dress with abstract floral patterns, sateen twill yoke and collar, red button, with matching cap edged in yellow stitching. The dress was originally sold with a belt (missing). It is a fabric variation of the Bleuette costume shown on the cover of this book and at right, and was advertised as being offered in various velvet designs. $500/700

34. "Cote d'Azur", the dress appeared in the Winter 1929/1930 catalog, made of soft blue wool flannel with fitted bodice, tapered waist, pleated skirt and cuffs, appliqué design, white feather stitch embroidery. $300/400

35. Dresser for Bleuette. Wooden dresser with metal frame, mirrored back, two large drawers and two handkerchief drawers, probably created for use with Bleuette. Circa 1925. $300/400

36. Bleuette, with bisque socket head, blue glass sleep eyes, mohair lashes, original Bleuette wig and pate, composition jointed body. The doll, 27 cm., is marked "Unis France 60 71 149 8/0" on the back of head, "8/0" on the front of throat,"2" on torso, and "1" on feet, and is wearing an original Bleuette costume "Parisienne" from the 1937/1938 catalog with cherry design on rich blue velvet with ribbed fabric weave, matching cap, chemise, Bleuette socks and leather shoes. The doll is from the 1925 era. $1200/1700

37. Original Bleuette catalog for Spring/Summer 1938 with cover and content illustrations by Manon Lessel in vibrant colors and amusing scenes. The cover illustration shows the elbow, knee and wrist articulation of Bleuette. $200/300

38. "Pierrot", the costume was shown in La Semaine de Suzette in February, 1922, comprising two piece Pierrot costume with black covered buttons and ruffled shirt, along with black silk Pierrot hat. Few brown spots on costume. $500/700

39. "On Dansera", the costume appeared in the Summer, 1932 catalog, comprising a sleeveless party dress of bronze green silk rayon with appliqué starched-silk cream and brown rosettes on the skirt and scalloped edging on the muslin-lined bodice. $500/700

40. "Chapeau Unique" from the Summer 1923 catalog, wire-framed hat made of tagal from palm trees, and trimmed with ostrich feathers. $400/500

41. "Grand Chic", the costume appeared in the Winter 1927/1928 catalog, comprising a black velvet coat lavishly trimmed with fur-like cuffs and collar, along with a matching muff, and a black velvet wide-brimmed hat. The ensemble reappeared in Winter 1936/1937 made in rose or blue wool. $500/700

42. Burnoose for Bambino of ivory silk with richly textured finish, fitted hood with silk banding that extends around the entire front of the cape, with silk ties. Circa 1930. $200/300

43. "Teddy", the hat appeared in the Winter 1918/1919 catalog, made of black silk taffeta with firmly shaped wide brim overlaid with ruched taffeta that is fringed at the edges, with self-piping and ruffled cap having fringed decoration at the top. $400/500

43A. Original Bleuette catalog for Winter 1918/1919, comprising four pages of delicate drawings and descriptions, with "Teddy" chapeau on the cover. $200/300

44. Fleischmann & Blodel Bleuette, with bisque socket head, dark blue glass set eyes, original Bleuette (very sparse) wig and pate, composition jointed body. The doll, 27 cm., is marked "6/0" on the back of head, "2" on torso, and "1" on feet, and is wearing white silk dress printed with bright red dots, with dropped waist hip sash, detachable lace bib, bonnet, undergarment, knit stockings and leather shoes marked "1". The dress is antique and may be originally made for the doll from unidentified Bleuette pattern. The doll is from the 1905-1915 era. $2200/2800

45. Original Bleuette Catalog, Winter 1937/1938, with cover and interior illustrations by Manon Lessel. The 12 colorful pages are amusingly conceived, ranging from Bambino's visit to a shoe store to Bleuette's pajama party. $200/300

46. Original Bleuette Catalog, Summer 1939 with cover and interior illustrations by Manon Lessel. The interior has 12 amusing illustrated pages with a variety of costumes for Bleuette and Bambino. $200/300

47. "Poids Plume" textured white nylon dress, appearing as #29 in the Spring/Summer catalog of 1956, the fabric was printed with abstract orange designs, has double flap decorations on the bodice trimmed with red buttons, detachable self belt, puffed sleeves. $200/250

"Orientale" shown in 1955 catalog of Gautier-Languereau.

48. "Orientale", the dress appeared in the Spring/Summer catalog of 1955, made of white linen-like cotton with paisley-patterned cotton bordering the skirt and forming collar and cuffs, attached white belt. $200/250

49. "Elle", the costume appeared in 1948, comprising a three-piece ensemble featuring jacket and bias-cut flared skirt of lime green linen-like fabric and a sleeveless white blouse. $300/400

"Uniforme" on left as it appeared in the 1936 Gautier-Languereau catalog.

50. "Uniforme", the costume appeared in the Winter 1936/1937 catalog described as "tres sobre, tres chic", comprising a navy blue dress with navy blue buttons, moleskin belt, polka dotted white collar and cuffs; along with a "Chapeau Breton" of navy blue pressed felt flannel with white band trimmed with blue polka dots. $400/500

51. Grey felt flannel cloche with royal blue twill banding decorated with three rhinestones. Unidentified. Circa 1920's. $200/300

52. Woven blue/grey nylon cloche in intricately shaded pattern. Circa 1920's. $200/300

53. Natural straw bonnet with rounded top and wide brim, decorated with green thread and blue flowers. Circa 1925. $300/400

54. Navy blue and white checkered cotton sailor hat, with black silk banding and streamers. Circa 1930's. $150/200

55. Blue/grey textured nylon dress with white cutwork collar and cuffs, moleskin belt with silver buckle. Circa 1918. $300/400

56. Bleuette, with bisque socket head, blue glass set eyes, original Bleuette wig and pate, composition jointed body. The doll, 27 cm., is marked "SFBJ 60 Paris 8/0" on the back of head, "2" on torso, and "1" on feet, and is wearing a vintage costume, possibly handmade from Bleuette patterns, identical in styling to "Passe-Partout" (see #67) of grey twill with green wool plaid trim, along with matching shift style dress and cloche, original undergarments, white knit stockings, white kidskin shoes marked "2". The doll is from the 1915/1918 era. $1200/1700

57. Red Woolen Plaid Burnoose, with intricately stitched lined shoulders, gathered cape, point-shaped hood with double flaps and a frame of tassel pom-poms. Unidentified, circa 1930. $300/400

57A. Original Bleuette catalog for Winter 1938/1939, with cover and interior illustrations by Manon Lessel, 12 pages. $200/300

58. "Christmas", the party dress appeared as costume #7 in the Winter 1933/1934 catalog, made of ecru lace with tulle sleevelets and trimmed with red velvet sash and bow. Although seemingly simple, the dress is neatly constructed with self-scalloped hemline. $400/500

59. Bleuette, with composition socket head, blue set eyes, fringed brows, open mouth, (not original) brunette wig, composition fully-jointed body. The doll, 29 cm, is marked "France SFBJ 301 Paris" on the head and "1" on the feet. The doll is presented in an original Bleuette trunk along with original Bleuette costumes: "Nocturne" chemise de nuit from 1956, "Au Concert" from 1958, white cotton sundress and matching apron printed with tiny roses, green woolen dress, red and white checkered dress, blue and white knit sweater. Circa 1955. $1200/1700

60. Original Bleuette catalog from Winter 1954/1955 with cover and interior illustrations by Manon Lessel, 16 pages. $200/300

61. Bleuette, with bisque socket head, blue glass sleep eyes, mohair lashes, original Bleuette wig and pate, composition jointed body. The doll, 27 cm., is marked "SFBJ 60 Paris 8/0" on the back of head, "2" on torso, and "1" on feet, and is wearing a vintage complete "Croix Rouge" costume comprising nurse's uniform, apron, veil with Red Cross emblem, along with navy blue cape, original undergarments, white knit socks, white kidskin shoes. The doll is from the 1922 era. $1600/2100

62. "Sérieuse", the coat-dress appeared as #11 in the Spring/Summer 1940 catalog, made of patterned rose wool with two peach colored buttons, white collar with red edging. The dress was also available in blue. $200/300

63. Woven cloche from "Le Coin de la Modiste" section of the Summer 1936 catalog, of natural and rose straw with narrow bands that allow for easy shaped fit. Circa 1920's. $200/300

64. "Quel Affreux Temps", the rainy day coat appeared as costume #13 in the Spring/Summer catalog of 1955. The rubber-lined woolen coat in blue and green plaid features a detachable capuchon hood and long flared sides. $300/400

65. Bleuette, with bisque socket head, blue glass sleep eyes, mohair lashes, original Bleuette wig and pate, composition jointed body. The doll, 27 cm., is marked "24 SFBJ 60 Paris 8/0" on the back of head, "2" on torso, and "1" on feet, and is wearing a vintage Scouting costume, "Jeannette" with blue cotton shirt, aqua neck tie, black twill skirt with suspenders, matching cape with arm holes, wide-brimmed hat, undergarments, black stockings, (not original) black boots. The doll is from the 1924 era. $1600/2100

"Jeannette" as it appeared in the Gautier-Languereau catalog.

66. "Passe-Partout", the coat appeared in the Winter 1931/1932 catalog, made of heavy blue velour trimmed with gold fringe edged by periwinkle blue stitching, with matching four-panel cap with upturned brim. $800/1100

"Passe-Partout" as it appeared in the original 1931 Gautier-Languereau catalog.

67. "Un Beau Voyage", the two piece ensemble appeared in the Winter 1928/1929 catalog comprising a tweed woolen coat with neatly shaped curved front panels, large patch pockets, faux cuffs, single button, and blue woolen velour lining. Along with blue felt flannel hat with blue woolen piping. The hat was described in the catalog as available in a variety of colors. $800/1100

69. "Moscovite", the ensemble appeared in the Winter 1916/1917 catalog and Winter 1918 catalog, comprising black thick plush coat with ivory silk lining, silver buttons. Along with matching muff with rope handle and tassel trim. $900/1500

70. "France", featured in Winter 1918/1919 catalog, of white wool flannel, the front-flap coat is trimmed with hip belt, blue cording, stitching and embroidery detail; with matching wide-brimmed hat edged in blue cord, with white flannel banding. $800/1100

"France" costume as it appeared in the Winter 1918/19 Gautier-Languereau catalog.

71. "Armor", from Winter 1956/1957 catalog, featuring a white felt flannel duffle coat with hood, flannel closure loops with buttons, scalloped edging. $300/400

72. White woolen short jacket with wide sleeves, maroon cross-stitch design, blue chain stitch outline on front of jacket and sleeve edges. Unidentified. $100/150

74. Original Bleuette catalog for Spring/Summer 1919, four pages with delicate drawings of the costumes. $200/300

75. Original Bleuette catalog for Winter 1919/1920, four pages of costumes including undergarments. $200/300

76. Original Bleuette catalog for Spring/Summer 1920, four pages of costumes with delicate illustrations. $200/300

77. Original Bleuette catalog for Winter 1920/21, four pages of costumes for skating, seaside, blustery weather, undergarments. $200/300

78. Original Bleuette catalog for Spring/Summer 1921, fold-out catalog with six pages of costumes including at home wear, sports, dressy, shoes, hats. $200/300

79. Original Bleuette catalog for Winter 1921/1922, eight page with wonderful illustrations of costumes and accessories. $200/300

80. Bleuette, with bisque socket head, blue glass sleep eyes, (replaced) auburn wig and pate, composition jointed body. The doll, 27 cm., is marked "Unis France 71 60 149" (head) "2" (torso) "1" (feet) and is wearing a vintage costume comprising light brown woolen coat with faux-pockets, brown velvet collar and buttons, matching cloche, undergarments, original brown leatherette boots. The doll is from the 1925 era. $1200/1700

81. Bleuette, with bisque socket head, dark blue glass sleep eyes, feathered brows, original (cropped) brunette wig and pate, composition jointed body. The doll, 27 cm., is marked "SFBJ 301 Paris 1" (head) 2 (torso) 1 (feet) and is wearing red woolen Petit Bob coat with four brass buttons, matching red woolen cloche, undergarments, socks, shoes marked "2". The doll is from the 1925 era. $1100/1400

82. "Petit Bob", the first version of the popular ensemble that appeared in the Winter 1931 catalog, comprising navy blue woolen coat, four brass buttons, stand-up collar, belted back with bottom pleat, matching four-panel cloche with roll-up brim trimmed with two rows of white cording. $200/300

83. "Petit Bob", identical to #82 except in scarlet red color, the wool with a ribbed pattern. 1931. $200/300

Interior page, 1936/37 Gautier-Languereau catalog with "Petit Bob" costume.

84. Original Bleuette catalog for Winter 1936/1937 with illustrations by Maggie Salcedo. 12 pages include costumes for both Bleuette and Bambino. $200/300

85. "Petit Bob", the second version of the classic ensemble, that appeared in the Winter 1953 catalog, of plum red wool with four brass button front, lapel collar, belted back with kick pleat, matching four-panel cloche with roll-up brim trimmed with two rows of white cording. $200/300

86. "Petit Bob", identical to #85 except in royal blue color. Few moth holes. 1955. $150/200

87. Original Bleuette catalog for Winter 1931/1932 with cover and interior illustrations by Maggie Salcedo, comprising 12 pages of costumes and accessories for Bleuette and Bambino. $200/300

Interior page, 1931/32 Gautier-Languereau catalog with "Petit Bob" costume.

88. "Confortable", costume #106 in Spring/Summer 1923 catalog featuring a brown heavy cotton linen-like coat with six-button bodice, open front, shaped back waist. Along with matching brown flannel wool beret. $700/900

89. "Averse", advertised in La Semaine de Suzette in May 1949, plastic hooded cape for rainy weather, with neck ties. Along with white rubber boots. $100/200

90. "La Rafale", rainy weather ensemble appearing in the Winter 1929/1930 catalog, comprising poplin twill trench coat in the classic style, with belt, along with matching hat and black leatherette boots with turned-own top edges of white kid. $400/500

91. Bleuette with Trunk and Trousseau, the doll with bisque head, blue glass sleep eyes, mohair lashes, brunette wig, pate, jointed composition body. The doll, 29 cm., is marked "Unis France 71 301 149 1 1/4" (head), and is wearing "A Croquer" dress of navy blue cotton with red and white rick-rack and buttons, white organdy collar, chemise, straw hat, white socks, white leather sandals. Doll circa 1935. In original Bleuette trunk with trousseau comprising red velvet "Allure", red woolen coat, brown woolen "Confortable" (few moth holes) with beret, yellow shirt, white smock dress, pink and white apron, navy blue cape. $1500/2200

92. "Esquimau", the costume first appeared in the Winter 1928/1929 catalog and the following year appeared on the catalog cover. The three-piece knit set comprises leggings with ankle straps and drawstring waist, sweater with fleecy trim at hips, neck, and cuffs, and cap with fleece edging. $400/600

93. "Toque Moscovite", from Winter 1916/1917 catalog, a Russian style hat of real fur. $200/300

94. "Mousquetaire", the hat appeared in the Winter 1923/1924 catalog described as a "gracious tricorn" of black velvet with wire frame, aqua silk lining, aqua twill streamers and band. $200/300

95. "Mousquetaire", another example of #94, lacking the aqua twill streamers and band, having ivory silk lining. $200/300

"Depart" costume as it appeared in the Winter 1954/55 Gautier-Languereau catalog.

96. "Depart", the costume appeared in the Winter 1954/1955 catalog, comprising woolen coat in grey and cream shadow-pane design, double-breasted front with six black buttons, two pocket flaps, black velvet collar, matching beret with black velvet ribbons. $300/400

97. "Jeannette" scout uniform, from Winter catalogs 1937-1940, comprising blue cotton shirt with flap pockets and white collar, short navy blue skirt with center pleats, navy blue cape with stand-up collar and arm slits, beret, brown leather belt with silver buckle, brown twill sack with leather straps. $500/700

"Jeannette" costume as it appeared in the Gautier-Languereau catalog.

99. "Sur Les Cimes", from Winter 1932/1933 catalog, elements of the ski set including multi-colored hand-knit turtleneck sweater along with matching hand-knit cap with lavish pom-pom. $200/300

98. "Altitude", from Winter 1939/1940 catalog, comprising red and blue hand-knit sweater, stocking cap, and mittens, along with blue knit ski pants with ankle straps and white cotton top. $300/400

100. "La Laï Tou" hat, featured in Winter 1936/1937 catalog, Tyrolean style red hand-knit cap with red pom-poms and black band. $200/300

"La Laï Tou" shown in 1936/37 catalog of Gautier-Languereau.

101. "La Laï Tou", from Winter 1936/1937 catalog, featuring hand-knit white sweater with red and green highlights and red tassels, green knit skirt, green knit mittens, and green leather purse with red berry embroidery. $500/800

Accessories, #101.

102. "Le Disque", the costume appeared in the Summer 1929 catalog comprising white woolen hand-knit sweater trimmed with red and navy blue symbol, white wool pleated skirt, white woolen beret. Also included is matching hand-knit white woolen beret with blue and red design, shown in the catalog illustration. $700/900

103. Bleuette, with bisque head, brown glass sleep eyes, brunette human hair wig and pate, jointed composition body. The doll, 27 cm, is marked "SFBJ Paris 1" on the head, "2" on torso, and "1" on the feet, and is wearing a hand knit orange and cream woolen ensemble comprising one-piece shift dress, cardigan, cap, long orange coat-sweater, (mended) woolen stockings, brown leatherette shoes. The doll is still preserved in its original cardboard shipping box with Gaultier-Languereau label on the lid, along with 1919 postmark. Circa 1920. $1500/2000

104. "Frisquet", the costume appeared in the Winter 1923/1924 catalog, described as hand-knit, the one-piece dress with cream borders, was made in a variety of colors, here in plum, with two white buttons at the back. $400/500

105. Three hand-knit sweaters and pleated wool skirt for Bleuette, each sweater a different style. The pleated skirt appears to be the model shown with "Armor" in the original 1955 catalog, but sold separately. 1950 era. $300/400

106. "Sur Le Cimes", the winter sporting costume appeared in the Winter 1932/1933 catalog, described as a Norwegian style two-piece ensemble comprising a jump suit with sleeveless white cotton top and diagonal weave blue woolen pants with fitted leg cuffs, along with matching high-neck jacket also of blue wool in diagonal weave. $400/500

107. Fleischmann & Blodel Bleuette, with bisque socket head, blue glass set eyes, original brunette wig and pate, jointed composition body. The doll, 27 cm., is marked "6/0" on the neck, "1" on feet, and is wearing "Elle" costume comprising white silk blouse garnished with lace and tiny blue embroidered dots, blue bias cut skirt, chemise, woven cloche with tiny flowers, socks, (replaced) white kid shoes. The second model of Bleuette appeared in 1905 until 1915. $1700/2300

108. Original Bleuette catalog for Winter 1939/1940 with cover and interior illustrations by Manon Lessel. 12 pages of costumes and accessories. "Elle" and "Lui" costumes are featured on the cover. $200/300

109. "Lui", costume (later re-titled "Petit homme") to match "Elle" costume described in #107, comprising silk blouse and blue linen-like shorts, along with baby rattle. $150/200

110. "Bon Appétit", costume for Bambino that appeared in the Winter 1952/1953 catalog only, featuring white pique baby jacket and bib with white rick-rack edging, green oilcloth bib labeled Bon Appétit! $200/300

111. "Beau Bébé", costume for Bambino, comprising blue polka dot cotton romper suit with cross-straps in the front, white cotton shirt with embroidered rolled collar. Late 1940 era. $200/250

113. Bambino, with solid domed bisque socket head, painted tan hair, rosy complexion, blue glass sleep eyes, composition baby body. The doll, 26 cm., is unmarked, and is wearing "Premiers Pas" costume comprising white pique jacket with blue buttons, matching cap with shaped crown, blue shorts, blue kidskin slippers. Doll circa 1935. $1000/1300

114. Bambino, with solid domed bisque socket head, painted tan hair, rosy complexion, blue glass sleep eyes, composition baby body. The doll, 26 cm., is unmarked, and is wearing original Bambino white angora pants, pink and white angora sweater and matching cap, white knit slippers. Doll circa 1935. $1000/1300

115. Pink angora knitwear, sized for Bambino, with ribbed detail at neck, cuffs and legs, along with matching stocking cap and ribbed stockings. 1930's. $150/200

116. Knitwear and slippers for Bambino, comprising set of hand-knit top and shorts, along with blue knit slippers, and blue kid slippers. 1930's. $200/300

117. "Feu-Follet", costume for Bambino, from summer catalog of 1957/1958, of white textured cotton printed with roses and bluets, rick-rack trim, elastic waist. $150/200

118. "Pitchounet", costume for Bambino first appeared in Spring.Summer 1951 catalog, of shadowpane delicate white cotton with smocking detail and belt. $150/200

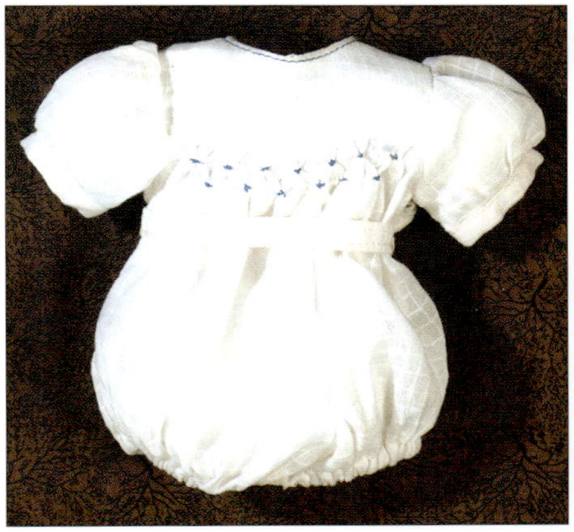

119. Romper suit for Bambino of pale blue pique printed with royal blue polka dots, with elastic leg openings, belt, pleated front. Along with white pique brimmed cap. 1930's. $100/200

120. "Burnous" for Bambino, from Winter 1930/1931 catalog, comprising fluffy plush hooded cape with blue cotton hood lining, angora trim edging, and a pair of matching slippers. $400/500

121. "Groënland", Bambino costume #34 from Winter 1954/1955 catalog, a two-piece ensemble of blue "jersey moltonne" with blue and white striped jersey hood lining and cuffs, along with matching mittens. $200/300

122. "Groënland", identical to #120 except in rich red color with red and white striped trim, along with matching mittens. $200/300

123. "Sur Les Cimes", costume #11 skiing ensemble from the Winter 1937/1938 catalog described as a one piece navy blue wool ski suit with zipper front and self belt. Included are wooden skis and ski poles with wrist and ankle straps, and boots. $500/700

124. "Megève", costume #1 from Winter 1953/1954, comprising red knit shirt with matching tasseled cap, and blue woolen overalls with bib front. The ensemble also appeared with blue shirt and maroon pants, and re-appeared as an ensemble for Rosette in Winter 1955/1956. $300/400

125. "Anorak", costume #1 from Winter 1950/1951, and for the two following winters, comprising hooded blue jacket with zipper front, and jumpsuit with white cotton sleeveless bodice and black woolen pants. $300/400

126. Original Bleuette catalog of 1953/1954, featuring "Megève" and "Groënland" costumes on its cover, in an amusing scene. $200/300

127. Original Bleuette catalog of 1936/1937 featuring "Sur Les Cimes" ensemble on the front cover illustration. $200/300

129. "Armor", costume #27 in the Winter 1956/1957 catalog, comprising a pale blue felt flannel hooded duffle coat with scalloped edging all around including the closure loops. "Armor" was shown worn with a pleated skirt and tall boots, and was offered in blue or white. $300/400

130. "Roland Garros", costume #24 from Spring/Summer 1955, one-piece white ribbed cotton play suit with cuffed short pants, sleeves, zipper front, button-back belt. $200/250

128. Bleuette, with bisque socket head, blue glass sleep eyes, mohair lashes, original brunette hair and pate, jointed composition body. The doll, 29 cm., is marked "71 Unis France 149 301 1 1/4" on the head, "2" on the torso, and "1" on the feet, and is wearing original yellow knit stocking cap with tassel, matching knit blouse, leatherette slippers and "Après-Ski" plaid woolen slacks that belong to her sister Rosette. She is walking two little Bleuette Scotty dogs with original leashes the dogs appeared in the Gautier-Languereau catalogs. Doll circa 1935. $1200/1500

131. Blue wool flannel jacket, possibly the jacket from "Trottinette", from Spring/Summer 1928 catalog, with four buttons, two faux pockets. $100/200

132. "Igloo", Bambino costume for Winter 1955/1956, comprising a one-piece blue cotton poplin jumpsuit with elastic at waist, cuffs and ankles, along with a matching elastic edge cap. The ensemble was listed again in the 1956/1957 catalog but noted as "sold out". $300/400

133. "Retour à La Terre", the costume appeared during the Occupation Years, in the Spring/Summer of 1942, featuring blue overalls with pockets, unusual self-belt and suspenders, along with plaid cotton sleeveless blouse. $500/700

134. "Capeline", the bonnet was offered in the Summer 1937 catalog, of variegated interwoven colors, able to be shaped. $200/300

135. Bleuette, with bisque socket head, blue glass sleep eyes, mohair lashes, brunette mohair wig, pate, jointed composition body. The doll, 27 cm., is marked "22 SFBJ Paris 60 8/0" on head, "2" on torso, "1" on feet, and is wearing "Paris Plage" costume comprising red shadow-pane play suit with little jacket, and straw cloche. The doll is from the 1922 era. $1200/1600

136. Bleuette beach chair "Atlantique" and beach bag. Wooden framed folding beach chair with striped canvas seat, along with canvas beach bag of cream, yellow and green stripes. The chair appeared often in the Bleuette catalogs. $300/400

137. Red espadrilles with rope soles and cream yarn trim and ties. The shoes first appeared in the Summer 1953 catalog. $150/200

138. "Le Lido", and other summer wear elements, comprising striped shorts, sleeveless vest with red edging, and green cotton chemisette with ribbon ties at the waist. 1958. $200/250

139. "Le Lido", illustrated on the cover of the Summer 1958 catalog, featuring a summer sportswear set of ribbed striped colors comprising vest and and matching shorts. $300/400

140. "Costume de Bain", from Summer 1923/1924 catalog featuring red cotton flannel two piece swim suit with white banding, middy style top, belt, matching cap with pom-pom trim, along with long cape with collar and neck ties (some minor spots on cape). The following year the costume name was changed to "Crevette". $400/500

141. "Clapotis", costume #28 in the Summer 1954 catalog, blue popeline swimsuit, elastic gathered for stretch-fit. $100/200

142. Bleuette, with bisque socket head, blue glass sleep eyes, mohair lashes, original mohair brunette wig and pate, jointed composition body. The doll, 27 cm., is marked "SFBJ 60 Paris 8/0" on the head, "2" on the torso, and "1" on the feet, and is wearing Mariner costume of 1920 comprising blue woolen pleated skirt and middy with black silk bow, cap with black silk band labeled "France", undergarments, white socks, white leather Bleuette shoes. The doll is from the 1918 era. $1800/2200

143. "Capri", costume #26 from the Summer 1954 catalog, featuring blue and white jersey top, along with red linen-like Capri pants with double pockets (pocket buttons missing); along with blue and natural straw woven sun hat shown in the catalog to be worn with the set. $400/500

144. "Capri", costume #26 from the Summer 1954 catalog, identical to #132 except blue pants, no hat. $200/300

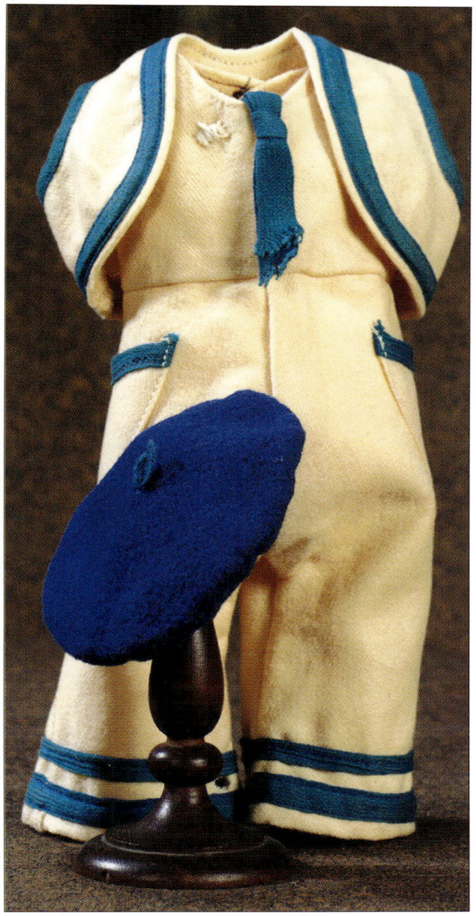

145. "Juan les Pins", appearing on the cover of the Summer 1932 catalog described as a "tres moderne ensemble" of beachwear, comprising a one-piece sleeveless suit with matching sleeveless vest, made of white cashmere wool, trimmed with blue twill edging and tie, with double pockets. Along with matching royal blue beret named "Chiquito". The ensemble also appeared in catalogs from 1933-1935. $400/600

146. Bleuette, with bisque socket head, blue glass sleep eyes, mohair lashes, original brunette mohair wig and pate, jointed composition body. The doll, 29 cm., is marked "Unis France 71 60 149" on the head, "2" on the torso, "1" on the feet, and has a paper label on torso Fabrication Francaise SFBJ. The doll is wearing summer season Mariner costume of 1919 of white twill with blue collar and tie, cap with blue band labeled "Guynemer", undergarments, socks, original Bleuette shoes. The doll is from the 1930 era. $1200/1600

147. Bleuette, with bisque socket head, blue glass sleep eyes, mohair lashes, blonde mohair wig and pate, jointed composition body. The doll, 27 cm., is marked with illegible letters (probably SFBJ) and "1" on head, "2" on torso, and "1" on feet, and is wearing Bleuette mariner costume from winter 1922, comprising red woolen middy with blue collar, blue woolen pleated skirt, blue cap with red pom-pom labeled Verdun, undergarments, white socks, black shoes. The doll is from the 1922 era. $1200/1600

145A. Original Bleuette catalog for Summer, 1935, with cover and content illustrations by Manon Lessel, comprising 12 pages of costumes and accessories for Bleuette and Bambino. $200/300

148. "Marin Reims", from Winter 1921/1922 catalog, the three-piece ensemble comprises dress with sleeveless cotton top, pique yoke with banding and pleated skirt, matching blue wool middy blouse and blue wool sailor cap with red pom-pom. The cap is lettered "Reims". $400/500

149. "Marin Reims" from Summer 1922 catalog, the three-piece ensemble comprises dress with sleeveless top and navy blue cotton V-shaped yoke, black woolen pleated skirt, red woolen middy over-blouse with black cotton collar, blue bow. Along with black cap with red pom-pom, white grosgrain trim, black silk banding labeled "Reims". $400/500

"Marin" shown in 1920 catalog of Gautier-Languereau.

"Marin" shown in 1920 catalog of Gautier-Languereau.

150. "Marin Foch", from Summer 1920 catalog, the three-piece ensemble comprises sleeveless dress with blue cotton yoke, black pleated wool skirt, red woolen middy blouse with blue cotton collar and black silk tie, black woolen sailor cap with red pom-pom. The cap is lettered "Foch". $400/500

151. "Marin", with white cotton short-sleeved middy blouse with blue collar and cuffs, white striping, navy blue tie, darkest navy blue woolen pleated skirt with button attachment. Mid 1930's. $300/400

153. "Marin", from Summer 1933 catalog, the three-piece ensemble comprises white woolen short-sleeved middy blouse with blue collar and cuffs, white striping, black silk tie, black pleated woolen skirt with button attachment, along with matching blue woolen cap with red pom-pom and navy blue silk banding. $400/500

152. "Marin Atlantic", from Winter 1952/1953, the three piece ensemble comprises white pique pleated skirt, white middy blouse with short sleeves and black grosgrain stripes, navy blue bow. Along with matching white cap with blue silk band labeled "Atlantic" in gold letters. $400/500

154. "Marin", from Summer 1933 catalog, the three-piece ensemble comprises white woolen short-sleeved middy blouse with blue collar and cuffs, white striping, black silk tie, black pleated woolen skirt with button attachment, along with matching white woolen cap with red pom-pom and navy blue silk banding. $400/500

155. "Marin Guynemer", from Spring/Summer 1919 catalog, the three piece ensemble comprises white pique middy over-blouse with black collar, white thread striping, navy blue bow, over matching sleeveless dress with black V-shaped bodice and pleated skirt. With matching cap with black silk banding labeled "Guynemer". A bit dusty. $400/500

156. "Marin Atlantic", from Winter 1952/1953 catalog, the three-piece ensemble comprises white pique middy over-blouse with navy blue collar and black tie, dress with sleeveless top and navy blue V-shaped yoke insert, pleated skirt. With matching cap labeled "Atlantic". A bit dusty. $300/400

"Marin" and other seaside costumes shown in 1923 catalog of Gautier-Languereau. On the right is "Juan Les Pin," #145 of this book.

156A. Bleuette type, composition socket head, blue glass sleep eyes, mohair lashes, (replaced) mohair wig, jointed composition body. The doll, 29 cm., is marked Unis France 149 251 2", and researchers differ on the Gautier-Languereau presentation of the model as Bleuette. The doll is wearing a white pique sailor suit, socks and brown shoes. The doll is from the 1950 era. $400/500

157. Bleuette type, bisque socket head, blue glass sleep eyes, real lashes, original brunette human hair and pate, jointed composition body. The doll, 29 cm., is marked "Unis France 71 251 149 2" and authorities differ on the Gautier-Languereau presentation of the model as Bleuette. The doll is wearing original Bécassine costume from the Winter 1917 catalog. The doll is from the 1930 era. $900/1300

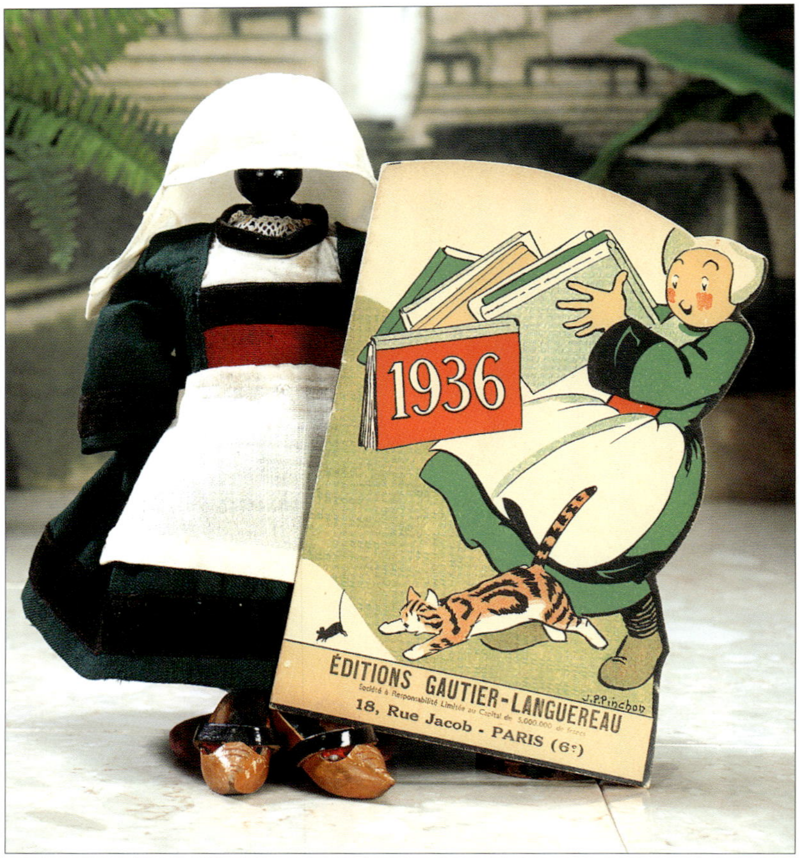

158. "Bécassine" costume, first appearing as a pattern in 1908 La Semaine de Suzette and then in the Gautier-Languereau catalog of 1916/1917, comprising green woolen dress with black velvet trim, red bodice, white apron and cap. Along with 1936 book catalog from Gautier-Languereau with die-cut design of Bécassine on the cover. $300/400

A humorous page featuring Bécassine shown in 1923 catalog of Gautier-Languereau.

159. Eight volumes of La Semaine de Suzette from the years 1921, 1923, 1926 (2), 1927,1930, 1933, 1937. $300/400

160. Bécassine, the soft cloth character doll with stockinette cover, button-shaped nose, painted eyes and brows, stitch-shaped hands, sewn-on red striped stockings and brown felt shoes, is wearing classic Bécassine costume of green and red wool, with black velvet bands, pantalets, with wicker basket. The Bécassine costume was offered in the Bleuette catalogs from their first issue, and this cloth version appeared in early issues of La Semaine de Suzette offered in several sizes. 48 cm. Circa 1940. $600/800

161. Original Bleuette catalog of Winter 1956/57 featured a cover illustration with Bécassine dolls, drawn by Manon Lessel. $200/300

164. "At Home", from the Spring/Summer 1925 catalog, featuring a turquoise linen-like peignoir with cream pockets, collar and cuffs, cream drawstring ties at the waist. $200/300

165. "Huit Heures", the pajama set first appeared in the Winter 1930/1931 catalog and continued to be offered for four additional years, of cream flannel with delicate rose striping, frog loop closure, pink cotton collar, cuffs and pant edges. $200/300

163. Bleuette, with bisque socket head, black enamel inset eyes, original (cut) blonde mohair wig and pate, jointed composition body. The doll, 27 cm., is marked "PR SFBJ 60 Paris 8/0" on head, "2" on torso, "1" on feet, and with original SFBJ label, and is wearing original Bleuette muslin chemise. The doll is from the 1917 era. $1500/1900

167. "At Home" Robe and Pajamas from Summer 1921 catalog, comprising a pale yellow pique bathrobe printed with delicate roses, with solid yellow collar, along with matching pajamas trimmed with orange edging. $400/500

168. Pajamas, Bathrobe and Slippers, the two-piece cotton pajamas of cream with pink polka dots and white braid trim, the contrasting robe of heavier jacquard weave has pink dots in different variation and wide twill banding and tie; and the pink corduroy slippers have black edging and pom-poms, from the late 1940 era. $400/500

169. Cotton pajamas, of linen like cotton with blue polka dots, Chinese style short jacket and 3/4 pants with V-shaped waistband. Circa 1950. $150/200

170. Three chemises, comprising short presentation chemise with lace trim, short muslin presentation chemise from 1933/1940 period; and chemise de nuit, presented from 1916/1934. $200/300

171. Two sleeping garments, comprising standing chemise de nuit of white cotton with lace edging, along with "Bonne Nuit" a one-piece combination with red galon trim that appeared in the Winter 1935/1936 catalog. $200/300

172. "Lingerie-Tablier", that appeared in the Bleuette catalog from 1916-1934, designed to be worn at the dressing table, of dainty fabric with lace edging and straps, silk ribbon ties. Few brown spots on lace. $200/300

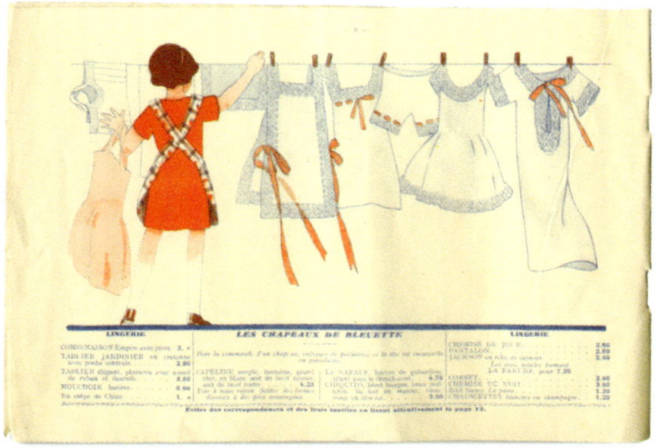

Lingerie shown in Winter 1931/32 catalog of Gautier-Languereau.

173. Blue presentation chemise printed with colorful flowers, being the last chemise of the Bleuette series, circa 1955. $100/150

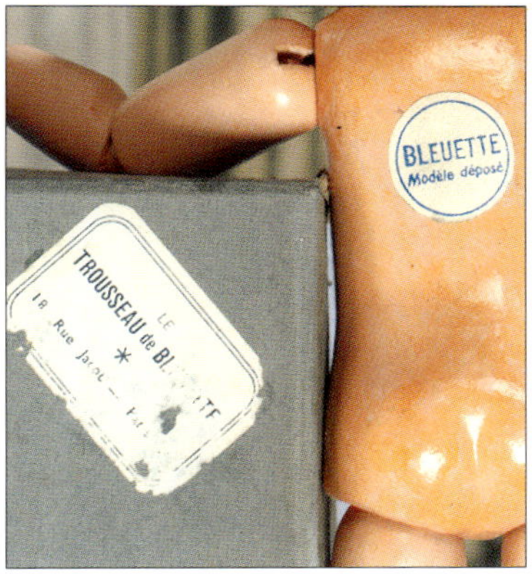

174. Bleuette, with bisque socket head, dark blue glass sleep eyes, mohair lashes, original brunette wig and pate, jointed composition body. The doll, 29 cm, is marked "71 Unis France 149 301 1 1/4" on the head, "1" on the feet, and "Bleuette Modele depose" paper label on back torso, and is wearing original blue flowered shift, and original socks and white kid shoes. The doll is presented in her original blue box with original label "Le Trousseau de Bleuette". The doll is from the 1930's. $1200/1800

175. Undergarment set, from 1925-1930, featuring full muslin slip with lace edging, with matching panties having lace edging and silk ribbons. $100/200

Lingerie shown in Summer 1933 catalog of Gautier-Languereau.

177. White cotton presentation chemise for Bleuette, the fifth model used during the 1940's. $100/150

177A. Muslin undergarments, the full slip with hip pleats and matching panties, each trimmed with delicate cotton lace, still stitched together. $100/200

176. "Parure Valisière", from the 1946 catalog, the pink rayon full-length night robe features elastic waist and sleeves, with original paper label "Valisière" of the famous French lingerie maker. Few small holes. $200/300

178. "Parure Valisière" from the 1940 catalog, comprising rayon nylon slip and panties, each with original paper label "Valisière" and panties with cloth label. $200/300

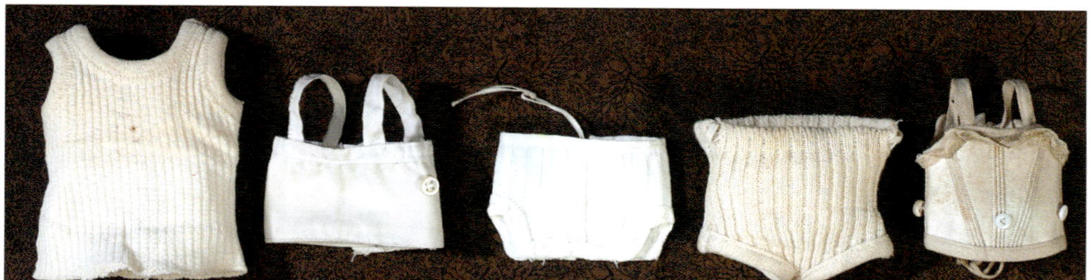

178A. Undergarments for Bleuette including knit shirt and pants, sateen stays, and two cotton stays. $100/200

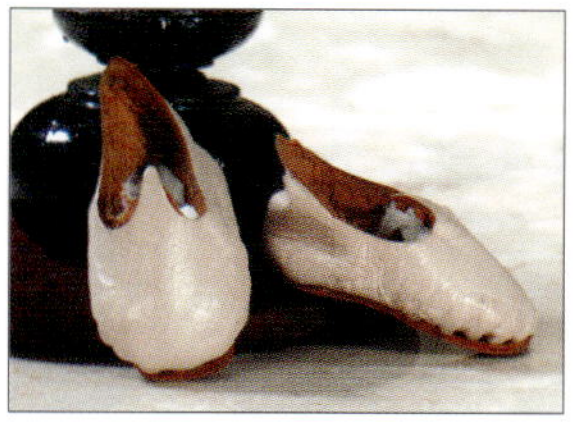

179. "Bien-Être", #5 in the Spring/Summer 1956 catalog, a robe de chambre made of soft rose cotton printed with flowers and spiral pattern. Along with matching rose kid slippers. $300/400

181. Blue muslin night gown with white crocheting on the ruched bodice and hemline, elastic waist with pink bow. Circa 1960. $100/200

180. "Petit Bateau", #6 from Winter 1955/1956 catalog, comprising knit sleeveless shirt and panties, original stitching together, "Paris" label in shirt. $200/250

182. Pink nylon half slip and panties with pleated and lace edging. 1955 era. $100/200

185. "Boutons de Rose", from the Winter 1955/1956 catalog featuring two-piece flannel pajamas with white flannel bottoms, and pajama top printed with little rosebuds ("boutons de rose"). $200/300

"Dolente" as appeared in the Winter 1954/55 catalog of Gautier-Languereau.

183. "Dolente", #4 from the Winter 1954/1955 catalog, peignoir of ivory ribbed velvet, with pocket and three button closure. $200/300

184. "Bien-Être", #4 from the Spring/Summer 1957 catalog, featuring a blue robe with ribbon-like pattern, having silky lustrous finish on the exterior and cozy flannel finish on the inside, white pearl buttons. $200/300

184A. Baptême Bonnet, appeared as #47 in the Winter 1916/1917 catalog, of peach silk crepe under fine organdy, trimmed with fine tulle lace and silk ribbons. The bonnet in different variations appeared in Bleuette catalog for several years and was one of the more expensive clothing items available. $200/250

186. (above left) "Le Beau Jour", first communion costume #15 from Spring/Summer 1952, comprising voile dress, bonnet, and veil garnished with lace and tucking, along with aumoniere and muslin underslip. Original finish, slight overall dustiness. $200/250

187. (above) "Le Beau Jour", first communion costume from 1937-1948, featuring white batiste gown with lace and tucks, full slip, veil, and silk twill aumoniere with braid trim and silk ribbons. $300/400

188. (left) "Le Beau Jour", communion costume from 1940's era, comprising batiste white dress with tucking on skirt, lace ruffle, matching full slip, veil and bonnet with matching lace to dress. Small spot on gown. $200/250

189. Bleuette, with bisque socket head, blue glass sleep eyes, mohair lashes, brunette wig and pate, jointed composition body. The doll, 29 cm., is marked "71 Unis France 149 60 1 1/4" on the head, "2" on the back torso, (lower legs repainted so mark not legible), and is wearing communion costume "Le Beau Jour" from 1949 period including dress, underslip, veil, cap, rosary, rosary case, aumoniere, socks. The doll is from the late 1930's. $1200/1700

190. Bleuette, with bisque socket head, blue glass set eyes, brunette human hair wig, pate, jointed composition body. The doll, 27 cm., is marked "1" on the head", "2" on the torso and feet, and is wearing early muslin chemise. The lower legs are not original. Circa 1905. $2000/2500

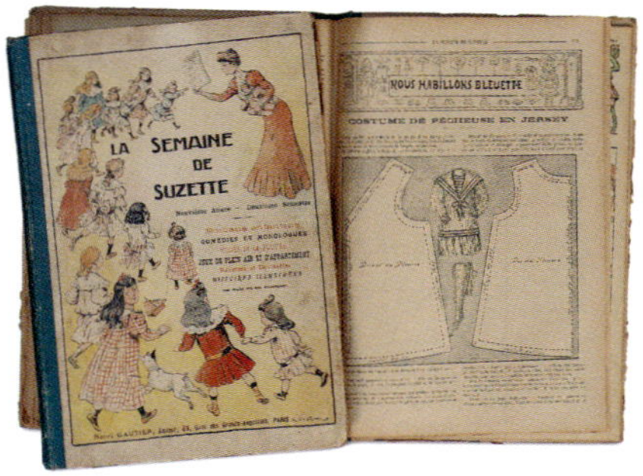

191. Two early bound volumes of Semaine de Suzette, from 1913 (neuvième année, premier semester) and 1914 (neuvième année, deuxième semester), with stories, monologues, modes de la poupée, little work sheets, recipes, patterns. $100/200

192A. Early lace bonnet of re-embroidered tulle with tatted cap top, double row of ruffles edged with ivory silk. The bonnet is probably "Brise" that was described in the Summer, 1921 catalog as complementing a lace summer dress. $300/400

192. Early lace dress of re-embroidered tulle with drawn-work high waist, rolled collar and cuffs edged with ivory silk, with ivory silk lining; the dress matches bonnet #192A, although its name is unidentified. Circa 1920. $500/700

193. White cotton dress with blue polka dots, possibly part of "Pastilles" ensemble of Summer, 1935. $150/200

194. "Vendanges en Champagne", costume #9 from Spring/Summer 1937 catalog, featuring blue and white cotton sleeveless sundress with pique collar, blue leatherette belt with silver buckle, matching sunbonnet with wide brim. $200/300

195. "Pimpante", of navy blue linen-like fabric printed with abstract red and white squares, silk twill neckline, bretelle sleeves. Circa 1940. $200/300

196. "Vendanges en Champagne", costume #9 from Spring/Summer 1937 catalog, a fabric variation of the dress shown here as #194, without sunbonnet. $150/200

197. "En Longs, En Large", dress from Spring/Summer 1952 catalog, of pink nylon stripes in blue, green yellow and white with horizontal tucks on bodice, white organdy collar. $300/400

199. Toque de Pailletine, from Summer 1931 catalog, shaded red woven bands with multicolored flecks, along with brown leather sandals marked "3". $200/300

198. Bleuette in trunk with trousseau, the doll with bisque socket head, blue glass sleep eyes, mohair lashes, brunette hair (cut) and pate, jointed composition body. The doll, 27 cm., is marked "1" on head, "2" on torso, and "1" on feet, and is presented in original Bleuette trunk with three undergarments including chemise embroidered "B", and five dresses including variation of Smocks, two variations of black bow dresses from after the war, unusual brown cotton dropped waist dress with pearl buttons, and cotton polka dot dress. The doll is from the 1915 era. $800/1200

200. "Rallye" for Rosette, #33 in the Winter 1958/1959 catalog, comprising sienna velvet dress with white pique yoke and pocket edging, along with cutwork linen-like slip for Rosette. $400/500

201. Bleuette Type, with bisque socket head, blue glass sleep eyes, mohair lashes, brunette hair and wig, jointed composition body. The doll is marked "Unis France 71 149 301 2" on head, "1" on feet, and is wearing original Bleuette chemise and straw cloche. $1100/1300

202. Rosette, with bisque socket head, blue glass sleep eyes, mohair lashes, ochre eye shadow, blushed cheeks, (replaced) brunette human hair braids, jointed composition body. The doll, 33 cm., is marked "71 Unis France 149 301 3" on back of head, and "3" on front throat, and is wearing original chemise. Circa 1955. $900/1200

202A. Green and red espadrilles for Rosette with rope soles and cream and yellow yarn ties and embroidery. The espadrilles first appeared in 1956. $150/200

202B. Sac with faux-tortoise rim, with amusing design in cotton fabric depicting two young googly type girls. A nearly duplicate model, with wooden handle, was shown in La Semaine de Suzette in June 1930. $200/300

204. "Smocks" from Summer 1939, costume #30, white pique dress with bodice smocking in orange and blue; according to the catalog description the color of smocking varied. $200/250

203. "Quatorze Juillet", costume #28 from Spring/Summer 1957, white cotton sundress printed with bursts of red and blue flowers, along with matching short cape and waist sash. The costume commemorated French Bastille Day. $300/400

Detail, #203.

"Smocks" shown in Summer 1939 catalog of Gautier-Languereau.

205. "29° à l'Ombre", #26 sundress from the Spring/Summer 1956 catalog, featuring a flowered cotton sundress with bows on the shoulder straps. $300/400

206. Seven issues of "Suzette en Vacances", 1933, 1934, 1936, 1937, 1938, 1939, 1940, published by Gautier-Languereau to accompany Bleuette activities. $200/300

207. Summer bonnet, unidentified model, with textured and patterned cotton cap encircled by black straw banding. Circa 1920. $200/300

26. 29° A L'OMBRE
Pour les grandes chaleurs, voici la robe idéale de fraîche cotonnade fleurie. Nœuds sur les épaules .... 250 fr.

27. ARLÉSIENNE
Robe de charmante cotonnade aux dessins provençaux, en jaune et vert, ou bleu et rouge, sur fond blanc. Une cordelière la resserre à la taille. 300 fr.

Attention... Nos toilettes sont exclusivement créées pour Bleu

8

"29° à l'ombre" shown in Spring 1953/54 catalog of Gautier-Languereau.

208. "Bien-Être" from Winter, 1951/1952 catalog, blue textured cotton robe with white pique lapel collar, and printed in abstract pattern of red, white and navy blue. $200/250

209. "Kermesse", from Spring/Summer 1957, costume #23, summer dress of large blue and white checkered print with red buttons and red rick-rack trim. $200/250

210. "Arts-Ménagers", the pinafore appeared as #6 in the Winter 1953/1954 catalog, of white cotton with blue polka dots, front closure decorated with two dark blue buttons. $200/250

211. "Arts Ménagers", from Winter 1953/1954 catalog, the pinafore of white cotton with large blue polka dots, two pearl buttons at front waist closure. $150/200

212. Pink cotton tablier with center pocket and red dot embroidery, unidentified, mid 1920's. $100/150

213. "Bulle de Savon", (Blowing Bubbles), #10 in the Winter 1954/1955 catalog comprising a pinafore apron with large center pocket, open back. $200/250

10. BULLES DE SAVON
Charmant tablier à poche centrale coulissée en imprimé de couleurs vives **198** fr.

★

11. MOTS CROISÉS
Classique tablier d'écolière en tissu coton à damiers bleus, rouges ou verts sur fond blanc .... **250** fr.

CARTABLE de cuir havane .... **140** fr.

★

12. ARTS MÉNAGERS
(redemandé)
Tablier coton pois rouges ou bleus sur fond blanc .... **215** fr.

★

14. LA VRAIE BÉCASSINE
(modèle déposé)
En tissu bourré, conforme à l'héroïne des albums, présentée dans son carton.

Sur 0 m 50 ..... **3.250** fr.
Sur 0 m 40 ..... **2.475** fr.
Sur 0 m 33 ..... **1.985** fr.
Panier .... **200** fr.
Petit parapluie ... **700** fr.
Grand parapluie.. **750** fr.
Prix d'envoi en sus **150** fr.
La même sans accessoires sur 0 m 20, fétiche pour l'auto ou la chambre **975** fr.
Port en sus .... **75** fr.

4

Various pinafores shown in the Winter 1954/55 catalog of Gautier-Languereau.

215. "Mon Beau Village", costume #15 in the Winter 1949/1950 catalog, comprising blue and white cotton checkered two-piece sundress with pleated skirt, and matching sunbonnet with pleated brim. Along with blue espadrilles. $500/700

216. Bleuette, with bisque socket head, blue glass sleep eyes, mohair lashes, auburn wig and pate, jointed composition body. The doll, 27 cm., is marked "Unis France 71 149 301 1 1/4" on head, "1" on feet and has torso label "Bleuette Modèle Déposé". The doll is wearing pale blue woolen dress "Tartare" with white embroidery on the yoke, pearl buttons, white woolen beret, undergarments, white socks, black shoes signed "2". The doll is from the 1935 era. $1600/2100

217. "Champs-Elysées", costume #16 from the Winter catalog of 1953/1954 featuring a rodingote coat of rose velour wool with pocket flaps, three pearl buttons, and "amusant chapeau" to match. $400/500

218. "Champs-Elysées", identical to #217 except in pale blue. $400/500

"Champs-Elysées" shown in Winter 1953/54 catalog of Gautier-Languereau.

221. "Villégiature", from Spring/Summer 1940, blue toile shantung coat with cream braid trim and three buttons. $150/200

222. "Villégiature", from Spring/Summer 1940, rose toile shantung coat with cream braid trim and three buttons. Small fabric tears in right sleeve. $150/200

219. "Favori", costume #1 from Summer 1934 catalog featuring a coat in ivory ottoman de soie with three buttons, rose soie collar and cuffs. Along with early unidentified rose bonnet with lace edging. $400/500

220. "Coupe-vent" cap from Spring/Summer 1928 catalog of hand-knit creamy white yarn; the hat was designed to be worn with the costume "Championne". $150/200

222A. "Patinette", from Winter 1924/1925 catalog, a dainty of delicate cashmere silk with woven edging, silk lining. $200/300

223. "La Danse", dress #34 in the Spring/Summer 1955 catalog featuring a white mousseline dress printed with pastel polka dots, with bretelle sleeves. $200/300

224. "Smocks" from Summer 1939, costume #35, blue pique dress with bodice smocking in darker blue and coral; according to the catalog description the color of smocking varied. The costume was offered from summer 1938 until winter 1940. $200/250

225. Pink print cotton dress with pink collar and cuffs, unidentified, possibly handmade, post WWII era. $100/150

226. "Sagesse", costume #2 in the Winter 1956/1957 catalog, as well as the following year. The apron was described as a charming fantasy, of pink and white checkered pattern decorated with "points de croix" in vivid tones. It was also available in blue and blue. $200/300

227. Pink cotton pinafore with pink patterned bib front, straps and pockets. Unidentified, circa 1925. $50/100

228. "Soigneuse", #2 in the Summer 1955 catalog, the costume was described as a "charming pinafore" in an unusual pattern design, with center waist suspenders and pleated skirt. $200/300

229. "Sans Façon" from Spring/Summer 1951, featuring a Scottish pink plaid sundress with matching bloomers in cotton cretonne. $300/400

230. "Mascotte", costume #25 from Winter 1955/1956 catalog, of Scottish plaid in delicate pastel shades of rose and blue, faux pockets on bodice, white organdy collar. $300/400

231. "Proteger", from mid-1920's from a series of tablier apron that appeared during that era in La Semaine de Suzette and Gautier-Languereau catalogs, of cream background printed with blue flowers, two pockets, bib front with straps. $100/150

232. "Pluviose", costume #19 from the Winter 1958/59 catalog, featuring a pink venilux hooded raincoat cape with arm slips, neck tie. $200/300

233. "La Prairie" from Summer 1941 catalog, brightly colored flowered pattern dress with white collar, with matching button-back hat. The costume was made in several fabric versions. $200/300

234. "Tablier Jardinier", from Summer 1930 catalog, a cotton double-sided apron in colorful abstract pattern with side buttons. $150/200

235. Red cotton dress with white pattern, white collar, detachable belt, resembling "La Roseraie" from Spring/Summer 1956. $100/200

236. Red cotton dress with white pattern, white collar, detachable belt, resembling "La Roseraie" from Spring/Summer 1956. $100/200

237. (bottom left) "Idée Chic", a simple cotton dress of the Occupation Years, 1940-1945, of white cotton with abstract pattern of blue, yellow and pin, with white pointed collar and detachable belt. $200/300

238. (bottom right) "La Prairie Emaillée", from Summer 1930 catalog, the cotton print dress with ribbed central panel and tiny red embroidered dots came in various fabric patterns. Fading spot at back of dress. $150/200

239. Bleuette, with bisque socket head, blue set eyes, brunette mohair (replaced) wig and pate, jointed composition body. The doll, 27 cm, is marked "22 D SFBJ 60 Paris 8/0" on head, "2" on torso, and "1" on feet, and is wearing "Fenaison" dress and bonnet, undergarments, knit socks, and brown leather shoes signed "2". A very faint hairline is at left forehead. Doll circa 1918. $1100/1600

240. "Fenaison", featured on the cover of Spring/Summer 1954 catalog comprising a cotton print dress printed with unusual flower pot design in colorful red, blue, green and yellow design, self belt, with matching cotton bavolet bonnet with long throat loop. $200/300

241. "Fenaison", featured on the cover of Spring/Summer 1954 catalog comprising a flowered cotton print dress with pleats falling from the dress yoke, white cotton collar, self belt, with matching cotton bavolet bonnet with long tie strings. $200/300

242."Fenaison", featured on the cover of Spring/Summer 1954 catalog comprising a cotton dress with unusual pattern of child with duck and puppy, in colorful pink and green on cream background, self belt, with matching cotton bavolet bonnet with long throat loop. $200/300

243. Blue cotton dress with flowered designs, pleated front, black velvet bows, along with matching bloomers, from the first collection created after WWII, 1946 issue of La Semaine de Suzette. $300/400

244. Pink cotton dress and bloomers, a duplicate to #243 except color variation, 1946. $300/400

245. "Gentillesse" as featured in the Summer 1949 catalog and in publicity in La Semaine de Suzette, of orange cotton patterned with white abstract flowers, bretelles, white collar. $200/300

246. "Double Emploi", from Summer 1950 catalog, of red cotton printed with birds and sunflowers, with bretelles and white collar. Some fading. $100/150

247. "Le Clan", from the Summer 1954 catalog, a three-part ensemble comprising peach silk-like blouse, Scottish blue plaid jumper with pleated skirt, and Scottish tam. $300/400

248. "Chiquito" beret of brown flannel wool with brown silk banding and streamers, along with faux alligator brown school satchel with straps, hankie inside. Late 1920's. $200/300

249. "Le Clan", costume #23 from Spring/Summer 1955 catalog featuring a white cotton poplin blouse with red wool Scottish plaid skirt and suspenders, along with white wool beret, described in the catalog as "classique ensemble". $400/500

250. "Soigneuse", a slight fabric variation of the costume shown in La Semaine de Suzette on December 2, 1948, comprising cranberry red dress with tiny dots and large dots, white rick-rack at the neckline and sleeves. The alternate pattern did not have the larger dots. $200/300

251. "A Croquer", #36 in the Spring/Summer 1958 catalog featuring a navy blue rayon dress with red and white rickrack and buttons, white collar. $200/300

252. Pressed red felt flannel cloche, closely resembling the grey cloche "Bonjour" of the Winter 1925/1926 period, with red banding. $150/200

253. Bleuette, with bisque socket head, black enamel inset eyes, brunette human hair and pate, jointed composition body. The doll, 27 cm. is marked "SFBJ 60 Paris 8/0" on the head, "2" on torso, and "1" on the feet, and is wearing "Croix Rouge" costume comprising white nurse's uniform, blue cape with white band embroidered with Red Cross, blue cape, undergarments, socks, black leatherette shoes. Circa 1918. $2000/2500

254.

257.

255.

258.

254. Original Bleuette catalog from Spring/Summer 1940, with cover and interior illustrations by Manon Lessel. $200/300

255. Original Bleuette catalog from Spring/Summer 1953, cover and interior illustrations by Manon Lessel. $200/300

257. Original Bleuette catalog from Spring/Summer 1954, cover and interior illustrations by Manon Lessel. $200/300

258. Original Bleuette catalog from Spring/Summer 1955, cover and interior illustrations by Manon Lessel. $200/300

259. Original Bleuette catalog from Winter 1955/1956, cover and interior illustrations by Manon Lessel. $200/300

259.

260. Original Bleuette catalog from Spring/Summer 1956, cover and interior illustrations by Manon Lessel. $200/300

261. Original Bleuette catalog from Spring/Summer 1957, cover and interior illustrations by Manon Lessel. $200/300

262. Original Bleuette catalog from Winter 1957/1958, cover and interior illustrations by Manon Lessel. $200/300

263. Original Bleuette catalog from Winter 1958/1959, cover and interior illustrations by Manon Lessel. $200/300

264. Original Bleuette catalog from Spring/Summer 1959, cover and interior illustrations by Manon Lessel. $200/300

265. Two original Bleuette catalogs, Spring/Summer 1959, and Winter 1959/1960, with cover and interior illustrations by Manon Lessel. $250/300

266. Bleuette, with bisque socket head, black enamel sleep eyes, brunette mohair wig (replaced) and pate, jointed composition body. The doll, 27 cm., is marked "SFBJ 60 Paris 8/0" on head, "2" on the torso, and "1" on the feet, and is wearing Bleuette lingerie. Circa 1918. $1500/2000

267. Bleuette valise and costumes, including original valise as advertised in Bleuette catalogs with original paper label "Le Trousseau de Bleuette", and with an assortment of costumes including "Armor", "Mon Beau Village" dress and bonnet, "Au Concert" along with hand-knit blue dress, Valisière rayon night gown, and others. The Bleuette catalogs urged the purchase of the valise, offering a special shipping price if ordered is the same time as a costume or doll. $400/500

268. Leatherette travel valise from Gautier-Languereau catalog along with three various costumes. Some costume fading and dust. $200/300

269. "Chiquito", from Winter 1928/1929 catalog, beret of tan wool flannel. $150/200

270. "Niniche", from Winter 1939/1940 catalog in the feature section "Le Coin de la Modiste", cap of brown felt flannel with brown silk twill bow and streamers. $200/250

271. Black woolen flat-top cap with wire-frame for shape, red cording, tie. Unidentified. $100/200

272. Bleuette, with bisque socket head, blue glass sleep eyes, mohair lashes, ochre eye shadow, brunette human hair over cork pate, jointed composition body. The doll, 29 cm, is marked "Unis France 71 129 301 1 1/4" on head, "1" on feet, and "Bleuette Modele depose" on paper label on torso, and is wearing original chemise and Bleuette slippers. Circa 1935. $800/1300

Detail, #272.

273. "Harmonie", costume #18 from Winter 1956/1957 described as "tres elegant", featuring pleated skirt in tennis flannel with red pinstripes, suspenders, and a matching bolero jacket with red "galon" embroidery. $300/400

274. "Le Bon Petit Diable" from Winter 1934/1935, comprising white cotton blouse, plaid woolen pleated skirt with suspenders, along with Scottish tam with red silk banding and streamers. $400/500

275. Blue cardboard suitcase with an invoice card from Gautier-Languereau, along with several catalog costumes including "Le Beau Jour" (missing slip and veil), chemise, Valsiere pink rayon night shift, pink nylon panties and half slip, blue and white checkered dress with red rick-rack, pajamas bottoms, pinafore, and pink and white checkered tablier with cross-stitch pattern. $300/400

276. Bleuette trunk, petite size with variety of Bleuette costumes, comprising early mariner costume with middy blouse and cap; three woolen hand knit sweaters, bébé stays and petticoat, red woolen coat, plaid woolen suit, cotton dress and bloomers from WWII era with amusing pattern, and collarette from catalog costume. Some wear to costumes, some are catalog pieces, several appear to be handmade. $400/500

277. Bleuette trunk, grand size with variety of Bleuette costumes, mostly appearing to be hand-made, vintage, from original Bleuette patterns, including three coats (one with fur collar), "Moscovite" muff, two original chemises, one panties, two pinafores, dress with matching jacket and two hats, Japanese style kimono, rose rayon party dress with ruching trim, and three jackets. $400/500

278. Suitcase with costumes for Bambino, including romper suit with card designs, blue polka dot romper suit with white shirt, "Chou-Chou" jacket and bonnet, knit undergarments, rubber pants, blue short pants, blanket, pique hat, and early batiste bonnet, along with carrying case for Bambino as described in original Bleuette catalogs. $400/500